DATE DUE 1/02

GAYLORD   PRINTED IN U.S.A.

GREAT RECORD BREAKERS IN NATURE™

THE GRAND CANYON
THE WIDEST CANYON

Aileen Weintraub

The Rosen Publishing Group's
PowerKids Press™
New York

Published in 2001 by The Rosen Publishing Group, Inc.
29 East 21st Street, New York, NY 10010

First Edition

Book Design: Michael de Guzman
Layout: Emily Muschinske

Photo Credits: Background Image on all pages, p. 15 © Jim Steinberg/Photo Researchers; p. 6 © George Bryce/Animals Animals; pp. 4, 7 © David Muench/CORBIS; p. 5 © Chase Swift/CORBIS; p. 8 © Bettmann/CORBIS; p. 10 © Joel W. Rogers/CORBIS; p. 12 (shale) © Michael P. Gadomski/Photo Researchers; p. 12 (granite) © Joyce Photographics/Photo Researchers; p. 12 (limestone) © E.R. Degginger; p. 15 © Andrew J. Martinez/Photo Researchers; pp. 16, 20 © Tom Bean/CORBIS; p. 19 (mummy) © Dewitt Jones/CORBIS; p. 19 (cliff dwellings) © Jay Syverson/CORBIS.

Weintraub, Aileen, 1973–.
    The Grand Canyon : the widest canyon / Aileen Weintraub.
       p. cm.— (Great record breakers in nature)
    Includes index.
    Summary: This book discusses the Grand Canyon, explaining the creation of the canyon and the scientific information obtained from the rock formations.
    ISBN 0-8239-5641-5
    1.Grand Canyon (Ariz.)—Juvenile literature. 2. Geology—Arizona—Grand Canyon—Juvenile literature. 3. Natural history—Arizona—Grand Canyon—Juvenile literature. [1.Grand Canyon (Ariz.)] I. Title. II. Series.

F788.W45 2000
979.1'32—dc21   00-039165

Manufactured in the United States of America

CONTENTS

1 A Natural Wonder 5
2 A Changing River 6
3 Exploring the Canyon 9
4 A Rainbow in the Canyon 10
5 Layers and Layers of Rock 13
6 Every Rock Tells a Story 14
7 Searching for Clues 17
8 People of the Canyon 18
9 A National Park 21
10 The Grand Canyon Today 22
Glossary 23
Index 24
Web Sites 24

4

A NATURAL WONDER

The Grand Canyon is one of the most amazing sights on Earth. The canyon is a huge, long valley cut into the Earth. The Grand Canyon is made up of rocks that are many different shapes and colors. It has steep cliffs, winding paths, and high peaks. The Grand Canyon is in the hot desert of northwestern Arizona. The width of the canyon ranges from one-tenth of a mile (0.2 km) wide in some places to 18 miles (29 km) in others. The canyon is also very long and deep. It is about 277 miles (446 km) from one end to the other, and one mile (1.6 km) straight down.

◀ The edges of the Grand Canyon are called rims. The North Rim is 8,200 feet (2,500 m) above sea level. The South Rim is 7,000 feet (2,134 m). The mountain bluebird, on this page, lives in the canyon.

A CHANGING RIVER

Would you believe that the Grand Canyon was created by a river? The Colorado River began carving out the canyon six million years ago. Large amounts of water carried about 500,000 tons (453,592 tonnes) of mud, sand, and gravel downstream every day. This **sediment** in the river acted like sandpaper on the land. Over time, the force of the water and the sediment carved out the canyon. The canyon continues to widen because of rain, wind, and changes in temperature. These forces **erode**, or wear down, the rock.

The Colorado River is 1,450 miles (2,334 km) long. It is the largest river west of the Rocky Mountains. ▶

◀ *The stripe-tailed scorpion lives in the Grand Canyon. Here, the mother is carrying her babies on her back. A scorpion can sting enemies with its tail.*

EXPLORING THE CANYON

Native Americans lived in and around the Grand Canyon for thousands of years. In 1540, Spanish explorer Vásquez de Coronado and his men were searching for gold. During the search, his men saw the canyon. In the mid-1700s, people began to make maps of this part of the world. Then in 1869, a man named John Wesley Powell and a team of explorers journeyed down the canyon. They studied the canyon for a long time. They wrote down information about the rocks, plants, animal life, and people living in and around the canyon. After Powell's **expedition**, people became more interested in seeing the Grand Canyon.

◄ *This photograph shows John Wesley Powell and a Native American guide in the Grand Canyon. Powell wrote about the rocks, plants, and animals that he saw there.*

A RAINBOW IN THE CANYON

The layers of rock in the Grand Canyon are like a rainbow. There are many different colors. The main color is red, but some parts are gray, green, and even pink. There are also some brown and violet-colored rocks. Some of these rocks have changed color over time. The Redwall **limestone** forms cliffs of rock around the middle of the canyon. It used to be gray, but **minerals** from other rocks have washed down over it and stained it a deep red in places. The canyon walls also change color because of different **environmental** conditions. Constant erosion changes the shape and look of the canyon. These many-colored rocks are a big part of why people visit this beautiful site.

As water, wind, and temperature wear away the rocks, new ones become visible. The canyon walls are always changing. ▶

Shale is formed when mud dries and hardens into rock. This piece of shale contains minerals that give it different colors.

Limestone was formed from the bones, shells, and teeth of sea creatures. This happened during a time when the land was under the ocean.

Granite is made from melted rock that has cooled below Earth's surface.

This rock is pink granite. Granite is just one of the rocks in the Grand Canyon that is made up of many different colors.

LAYERS AND LAYERS OF ROCK

Scientists have discovered a lot about planet Earth by studying the Grand Canyon. The rocks in the canyon are from many different time periods. The oldest rocks are at the bottom. There is a layer of rock that contains **granite** at the bottom of the canyon. This layer is about two billion years old. Above that layer there are different types of rocks, including limestone and **shale**. These rocks are more than 500 million years old. The next layer is over 300 million years old. There were times when layers of the canyon were washed away. This is why some layers seem to be missing.

◄ *Much information can be learned about the history of planet Earth by studying the rocks in the Grand Canyon.*

EVERY ROCK TELLS A STORY

The rocks in the Grand Canyon tell us what the environment used to be like in the area. Limestone is a type of rock formed underwater. If you look carefully at the limestone in the canyon, you might see seashells. This is because this rock is made of the bones, teeth, and shells of dead sea creatures. This tells us that the Grand Canyon was once part of a sea. **Sandstone** is another type of rock found in the canyon. This rock is made out of **compacted** sand found in deserts or beaches. These layers tell us that at times the canyon was underwater and at times it was a desert. Shale is a type of rock formed by mud. When shallow water covered the land, it left behind mud that hardened into rock.

This piece of limestone is filled with the shells of sea creatures.

SEARCHING FOR CLUES

The rocks in the Grand Canyon give us clues about what kinds of plants and animals lived in the area. Many rocks contain different kinds of **fossils**. A fossil is the hardened remains of a plant or animal. A fossil can also be a rock that has the shape of a plant or of an animal's body marked on it. The fossils in the canyon change from east to west. In the east it is possible to see fossils of clams and snails. They lived in shallow water. As you move west, you can see fossils of the kinds of animals that might have lived in deep ocean waters, such as large fish. This is why scientists believe that there was once more water in the western part of the canyon.

◀ *These fossils are from sea animals that lived in the Grand Canyon millions of years ago.*

PEOPLE OF THE CANYON

Scientists have found many **artifacts** in the Grand Canyon. These artifacts, including dolls and carved figures, belonged to people who lived in the area over 4,000 years ago. A Native American group called the Ancestoral Puebloan lived in the area about 2,000 years ago. People have found the remains of their homes, called cliff dwellings. These shelters were built on or near cliffs. Scientists think that the Ancestoral Puebloan left because the weather became too hot and it was hard to grow food. The Havasupai are the only Native Americans that still live in the canyon. There are, however, other groups that live on nearby **reservations**.

Ancestral Puebloan people lived in cliff dwellings like these. The mummy of an Ancestral Puebloan woman was found near the Grand Canyon. ▶

A NATIONAL PARK

In 1919, the United States government made a large part of the Grand Canyon into a national park. This was done to protect the environment of the canyon. The government has paved roads along the rims of the canyon to make it easier for people to travel. There are also trails leading down into the canyon. Some of these trails are very narrow. One of the most popular trails that crosses the canyon from the North Rim to the South Rim is called the Kaibab Trail. A fun way to travel on these trails is by mule. Mules carry visitors through the canyon. Many people hike down into the canyon on foot. Others take boats down the Colorado River, which still cuts through the canyon.

◀ *National Park guides can tell visitors many interesting facts about how the canyon was formed.*

THE GRAND CANYON TODAY

The rocks of the Grand Canyon tell a wonderful story about how Earth changes over time. Many plants and animals now live in and around the canyon, where once there were very few. There are coyotes, foxes, deer, and even kangaroo rats living throughout the canyon. There are forests of pine, fir, and spruce on the North Rim. The South Rim is hotter and drier. It has plants that need less water, such as cactus and yucca. The Colorado River continues to break away pieces of rock from the bottom of the canyon. Harsh weather still wears down the rocks. This makes the canyon deeper and wider. We can only wonder what the Grand Canyon will look like in another million years.

GLOSSARY

artifacts (AR-tih-faks) Objects created or produced by humans.

compacted (com-PAK-ted) Packed together tightly.

environmental (en-VY-urn-ment-al) Having to do with the living things and conditions that make up a place.

erode (ih-ROHD) To wear away slowly.

expedition (ek-spuh-DIH-shun) A trip for a special purpose, such as a scientific study.

fossils (FAH-sils) The hardened remains of dead animals or plants that lived long ago.

granite (GRAH-nyt) Melted rock that cooled and hardened beneath Earth's surface.

limestone (LYM-stohn) Rock made of tightly-packed shells, bones, and teeth of sea creatures.

minerals (MIH-ner-ulz) Natural ingredients from Earth's soil that are not plants or animals.

reservations (reh-zer-VAY-shunz) Areas of land set aside by the government for Native Americans to live on.

sandstone (SAND-stohn) Rock made of tightly-packed sand.

sediment (SEH-dih-ment) Gravel, sand, silt, and mud that is carried by water.

shale (SHAYL) Rock that is made of hardened mud or clay.

INDEX

A
artifacts, 18

C
Colorado River, 6, 22
Coronado,
Vásquez de, 9

D
desert, 5, 14

F
fossils, 17

G
granite, 13

L
layers, 10
limestone, 10, 13, 14

N
Native Americans,
9, 18
National Parks, 21

P
Powell, John
Wesley, 9

R
reservations, 18

S
sandstone, 14
sediment, 6
shale, 13, 14

T
trails, 21

WEB SITES

To learn more about the Grand Canyon, check out these Web sites:

http://www.grand.canyon.national-park.com/

http://www.pbs.org/wgbh/amex/canyon/